W9-CTO-002

The Young Patriot's

REPRODUCIBLE

AGES 7-12

Book of Puzzles, Games, Riddles, Stories, Poems, and Activities

by CAROLE MARSH

The Young Patriot's Team

Carole Marsh • Michael Longmeyer • Diana Sullivan • Chad Beard • Terry Briggs • Billie Walburn • Cecil Anderson • Victoria DeJoy • Steven Saint-Laurent

Published by

GALLOPADE™
INTERNATIONAL

800-536-2GET
www.gallopade.com

Gallopade is proud to be a member of these educational organizations and associations:

NSSEA

The Unity of Our Nation...

Cut out and tape together. Proudly display your United States Flag!

The stripes on our flag represent the 13 original colonies and the stars represent our 50 states.

The Colors of a Country

I am America.
I am wrapped in red, white, and blue
From my mountains in their purple majesty,
To the oceans in every blue-green hue.

I am America
With my fields of waving, golden grains,
My dark green forests,
And clean white rains.

I am America
I am people—
Red, yellow, brown, black, and white.
I am people—
Medium, dark, and light.
I am every religion, every heritage, every race.
I am honor.
I am dignity.
I am pride.
I am grace.

I am America.

Activity:
Write your own patriotic poem!

_____

_____

_____

_____

_____

_____

America the Beautiful!

O beautiful for spacious skies,

For amber waves of grain,

For purple mountain majesties

Above the fruited plain!

America! America!

GRACE

God shed his grace on thee

And crown thy good with brotherhood

From sea to shining sea!

I ♥ the USA

Trace, color, cut out, and wear your patriotic button!

Fifty Nifty States!

Can you match them all?
Write each state's two letter abbreviation in the correct place on the map.
How many do you know?

Alabama–AL
Alaska–AK
Arizona–AZ
Arkansas–AR
California–CA
Colorado–CO
Connecticut–CT
Delaware–DE
Florida–FL
Georgia–GA
Hawaii–HI
Idaho–ID
Illinois–IL
Indiana–IN
Iowa–IA
Kansas–KS
Kentucky–KY
Louisiana–LA
Maine–ME
Maryland–MD
Massachusetts–MA
Michigan–MI
Minnesota–MN
Mississippi–MS
Missouri–MO

Montana–MT
Nebraska–NE
Nevada–NV
New Hampshire–NH
New Jersey–NJ
New Mexico–NM
New York–NY
North Carolina–NC
North Dakota–ND
Ohio–OH
Oklahoma–OK
Oregon–OR
Pennsylvania–PA
Rhode Island–RI
South Carolina–SC
South Dakota–SD
Tennessee–TN
Texas–TX
Utah–UT
Vermont–VT
Virginia–VA
Washington–WA
West Virginia–WV
Wisconsin–WI
Wyoming–WY

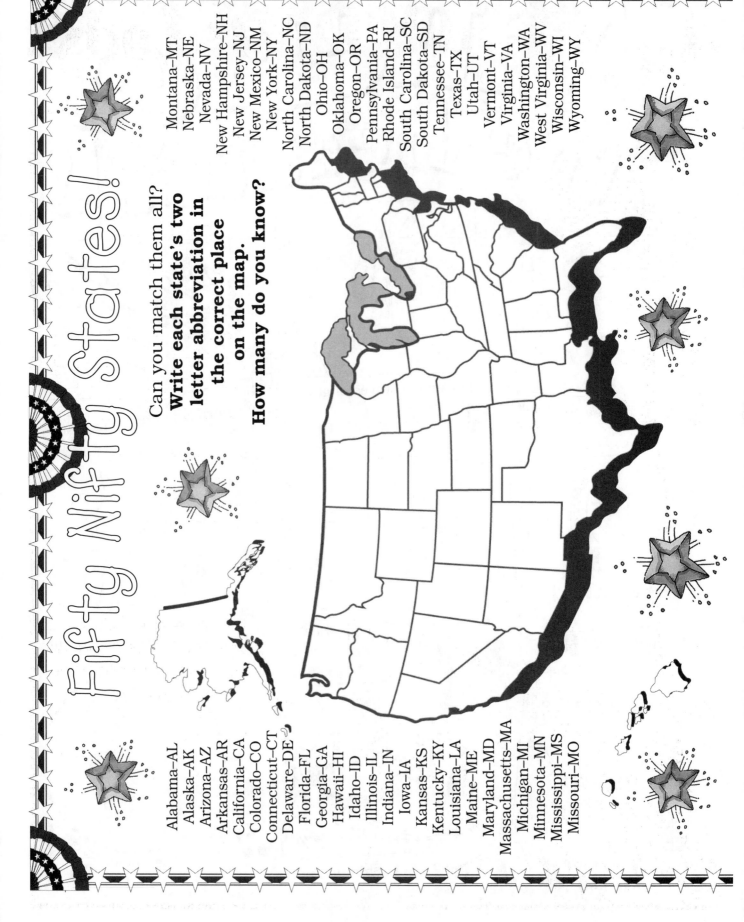

The Statue of Liberty was a gift from another country. Starting with the first letter, scratch out every other letter to learn which country.

G F I R K A O N X C Q E

The Statue of Liberty was so big that she had to be shipped in
___ ___ ___ crates.
To find the number, add 200 + 10 + 4.

Statue of Liberty

To reach the top of the Statue of Liberty, you have to climb

```
    192   steps in the pedestal
+   162   steps inside
+    54   ladder rungs to the torch tip
------
= _____   steps in all!
```

The Statue of Liberty arrived in pieces in 1876. In 1886, Americans held a big party to celebrate that she was finally all together!
How many years did it take to put her together?
1886 - 1876 = ___ ___ years!

Red, White, Blue, and You!

On September 11, 2001, the United States experienced one of the worst tragedies in its history. But, some good has come out of this bad event. Americans have joined together to make our country stronger. People have given their money, their time, even their blood! You may be "just" a kid, but there are things you can do too!

Kristen and Kayla sold homemade cookies: $12.54

Wade and Ellen made and sold red, white, and blue ribbon pins: $22.00

Katie cleaned under the sofa cushions and found: 89¢

Grant and Max washed their neighbor's car: $5.00

Miles gave his allowance: $3.50

Megan donated her ice cream money: 75¢

A lot of kids have collected money to send to a good cause like the American Red Cross. The total amount of their contribution is

$___ ___. ___ ___

Democracy is...

A democracy is a government where the people have a say in who their governmental officials are and what laws are made that will affect them—government <u>for</u> the people <u>by</u> the people. What does democracy mean to you? Using each of the letters in the word "democracy," write a word or phrase that describes democracy. The first one is done for you.

D is for <u>Debate</u>

E is for _____

M is for _____

O is for _____

C is for _____

R is for _____

A is for _____

C is for _____

Y is for _____

Red, White, and Blue Rainbow

Rainbows are a symbol of hope. After the storm comes the rainbow. America has a bright future.
So let those colors shine!

Color your own rainbow flag in patriotic colors!

The Pledge of Allegiance

...to Color, Say, and Display

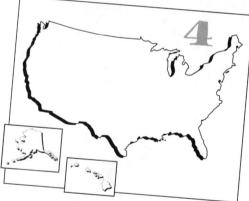

1

"I pledge allegiance

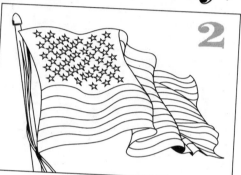

2

to the Flag of the
United States of America

3

and to the Republic for
which it stands:

4

one nation
under God, indivisible,

5

with liberty

6

and justice

7

for all."

The word
indivisible means
"a whole"

Scrapbook of...

Here are some pictures of beautiful places to visit in America. Have you ever seen any of them up close? Perhaps you can do that soon. Take your own pictures of the beauty of America and make a scrapbook. It's a fun, creative way to spend time with your family! Here are two spaces to get started.

Thomas Jefferson's Monticello, Virginia

Golden Gate Bridge, San Francisco, California

Statue of Liberty, New York

Cliff Palace, Colorado

American Pride

Look at the pictures on this page. Can you name the states where these three great American landmarks are located? Write your answers in the blanks below.

A. __ __ __ __ __ __ __ __ __ __ __

B. __ __ __ __ __ __   __ __ __ __ __ __

C. __ __ __ __ __ __ __ __ __ __ __ __ __

A

Gateway Arch, St. Louis

B

Mount Rushmore, near Rapid City

C

Space Needle, Seattle

Proud To Be An American!

Your friends and family are a special part of what it means to be an American. As Americans, we have many freedoms that people in other countries do not enjoy. Write a letter to a friend or family member expressing what being an American really means to you. Write about things you are thankful for. Write about your heritage. Write a poem. It's up to you!

A Symbol of Pride and Strength!

The American bald eagle is the perfect symbol of American strength, beauty, and pride.

How many eagles can you find nesting on the mountain?

_____

Did you know that Benjamin Franklin suggested that the turkey be our national symbol? Can you believe that?!

She's a Grand Old Flag

The flag is a symbol of our nation. To show our patriotism for our country, we pledge allegiance to our flag, and our nation for which it stands! When we see Old Glory waving in the wind, it is easy to be proud to be an American!

```
A  L  L  E  G  I  A  N  C  E
N  E  S  Q  F  T  M  V  W  B
A  S  T  R  I  P  E  S  H  W
T  Z  A  G  L  O  R  Y  I  A
I  C  R  P  X  M  I  M  T  V
O  B  S  R  E  D  C  B  E  I
N  Y  B  L  U  E  A  O  J  N
P  L  E  D  G  E  F  L  A  G
```

WORD BANK
ALLEGIANCE
AMERICA
BLUE
FLAG
GLORY
NATION
PLEDGE
RED
STARS
STRIPES
SYMBOL
WAVING
WHITE

One of the flag's nicknames is "Old Glory"!

There are ☐ red stripes.   There are ☐ white stripes.   There are ☐ stars .

All-American Fireworks!

Have you ever wondered how fireworks became an Independence Day tradition? The earliest settlers brought fireworks to the New World, where firings of black powder were used to mark holidays and frighten the natives! The first Independence Day was celebrated on July 4, 1777. By the early 1800s, fireworks were a part of the tradition!

Use your crayons, chalk, or gel pens to make your own "fireworks" in the night sky.

A Most Amazing Patriot!

Unscramble the words to uncover some little known facts about one of the greatest leaders in American history!

He made a **YRLSAA** of $25,000 per year.

_____

Washington was the first president whose likeness appeared on a **STGEPOA MPTSA.**

_____

George did not have a **LEDDIM** name or **NITILAI.**

_____   _____

He worked as a **URYSRVEO** in his younger years.

_____

Many believe that he never actually cut down the **HEYRRC** tree.

_____

Washington never had a pair of **DNEOOW** teeth.

_____

One of George's favorite menus included cream of peanut soup, mashed sweet potatoes with coconut, string beans with mushrooms, and Martha Washington's special cake. Mmm...Doesn't that sound good?

America's military forces are the most powerful and well-trained in the world!
Our military is a big part of what makes our country great!

These Colors

Don't Run!

Don't Tread on Me!

A symbol is one thing that stands for something else. For example, the snake on the flag to the right represents the American colonies. They were tired of being bossed around and taxed by England. Colonists flew this flag during the American Revolution as a message to the English. Don't tread (walk) on me. I will bite you!

Think of a symbol that represents you.
Design a flag to hang on the door of your room.

United States Symbols
SCRAMBLE

Write the number next to the name of these United States symbols.

____ Bald eagle   ____ Stars and Stripes   ____ Liberty Bell

____ Uncle Sam   ____ Statue of Liberty

The Joke's On You!

STAR: Did you know that the song "God Bless America" is meant to be sung at night?
STRIPE: No, how did you decide that?
STAR: Because it says that God should "stand beside her and guide her through the night with a light from a bulb!"
STRIPE: Oh, brother!

Q: What colors are in the American flag when it is waving in the wind?
A. Red, white, and blew!

A teacher asked her class if anyone knew what the capital of the United States is. Little Johnny raised his hand, "I know! It's Washington, D.C."

"Very good, Johnny!" the teacher said. "Now, do you know what the D.C. stands for?"

"Of course," said Johnny. "Dot com!"

Q. What did Ben Franklin's mom tell him to do when he was a little boy?
A. Go fly a kite!

Q. What does USA stand for?
A. US All

Q. What do pigs do on the Fourth of July?
A. In the pen dance. (GET IT? Independence!)

United We Stand!

On October 2, 2001, the U.S. Postal Service released a new stamp to show the renewed sense of patriotism many Americans have experienced. It is called the "United We Stand" postage stamp and shows a beautiful flag waving behind that important phrase.

In the past, the United States has had other patriotic stamps. A recent one featured the Statue of Liberty. There has also been one with Uncle Sam's picture.

UNCLE SAM WANTS YOU to design a patriotic stamp of your own!

THE STORY OF
STAR SPANG

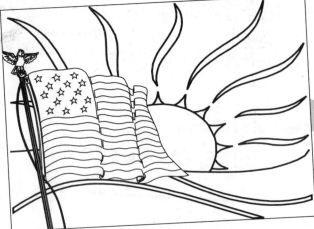

1 Oh, say can you see
By the dawn's early light

2 What so proudly we hailed
At the twilight's last gleaming

4 O'er the ramparts we watched
Were so gallantly streaming

5 And the rockets' red glare...
The bombs bursting in air...

7 Oh, say does that star
spangled banner yet wave....

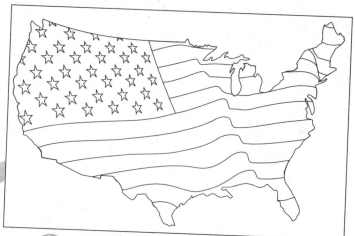

8 O'er the land of the free....

3

Whose broad
stripes and
bright stars
Through the
perilous fight

6

Gave proof
through the
night
That our
flag was
still there

9 And the home of the brave!

The original star spangled banner was the inspiration for the song written by Francis Scott Key that has become our national anthem.

Who made the flag?
Mrs. Mary Young Pickersgill and her daughter, Mrs. Caroline Purdy

When was it made?
July and August 1813

Where was it made?
Baltimore, Maryland

How was it made?
By hand—sewn with linen thread

Who paid for the work?
United States Government. Commodore Joshua Barney and General John Stricker of the Maryland Militia asked Mrs. Pickersgill to make the flag

How much did it cost?
$405.90

How big was the flag?
30 by 42 feet! The stars were two feet in diameter, the blue union was 16 by 20 feet, and the stripes were each 2 feet wide!

How much fabric did it take?
Four hundred yards of first quality single-play 18-inch woolen bunting

Where did the flag fly?
Over Fort McHenry during British siege in the War of 1812

How many stars and stripes did it have?
Fifteen stars and fifteen stripes—one for each state at that time

Where is the flag now?
At the Smithsonian Institution in Washington, D.C.

Dear Diary

Perhaps you have been in the stands singing the Star-Spangled Banner at a baseball game...watched a Fourth of July parade...placed flowers at a memorial...seen an air show at a military base. Many experiences can make us feel positive about being a part of this great country of ours. Recall your feelings on a special occasion and write them down!

Dear Diary

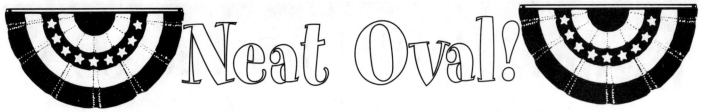

Neat Oval!

No doubt about it, the Oval Office would be one neat place to work!
The first oval office was built in 1909. Located in the West Wing, this is the most important room in the White House!
The President is allowed to decorate the Oval Office as he or she chooses. Imagine you are the president!
Decorate the office below with your favorite things and colors.

Earning Points for the USA!

This page shows some of the highlights you can see in our nation's capital, Washington, D.C. You can remove this page and use it as a game board. To play, get a coin or other type marker. Toss it at the page and be sure and note the points on the item where the coin lands. After 10 tosses, add the points and see how many points you have. Challenge a friend and see who gets the most patriotic points!

Washington Monument
10
POINTS

National Zoo
5
POINTS

Smithsonian Institution
2
POINTS

Lincoln Memorial
4
POINTS

Capitol Hill
5
POINTS

Library of Congress
3
POINTS

White House
10
POINTS

All-American Art!

One way to express your patriotism is making All-American Arts and Crafts! Check out this cool "colonial" craft.

According to legend, in June of 1776, George Washington asked Betsy Ross to make a flag for the 13 colonies. He wanted the stars on the flag to have six points. Betsy showed him a trick for easily cutting out stars with five identical points. Get your supplies ready and give it a try:

FIVE-POINTED STARS!

Here's how to make Betsy's five-pointed stars:

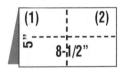

STEP 1

Fold an 8-1/2-by-10-inch piece of paper in half. Leave it folded and then fold it in half from top to bottom and again from side to side. When you unfold it, you should see a cross.

STEP 2

Take the upper left corner (1) and fold it from the center of the top to the crease on the horizontal line. Now take corner 1 and fold it back to the left until it lines up with the left side.

STEP 3

Take the top right corner (2) and fold it over to the left. Then bring corner 2 back to the right and fold it again. The paper now looks a little like a necktie.

STEP 4

With scissors, make a cut from corner 2 across the paper to a point about 1 inch down from the top point. When you unfold this snippet it should be a perfect five-pointed star just like Betsy made!

A FLAG OF YOUR OWN!

Use paper, and crayons, markers, or paints to design a flag of your own. It can represent America or just you. When you're finished, attach it to a pencil or stick with tape. Have a flag parade with friends or classmates!

America's Finest!

We are protected by our armed forces. In the air, on the land, and on the sea, America's military is the best!

Draw faces and other details on the military personnel, then color them!

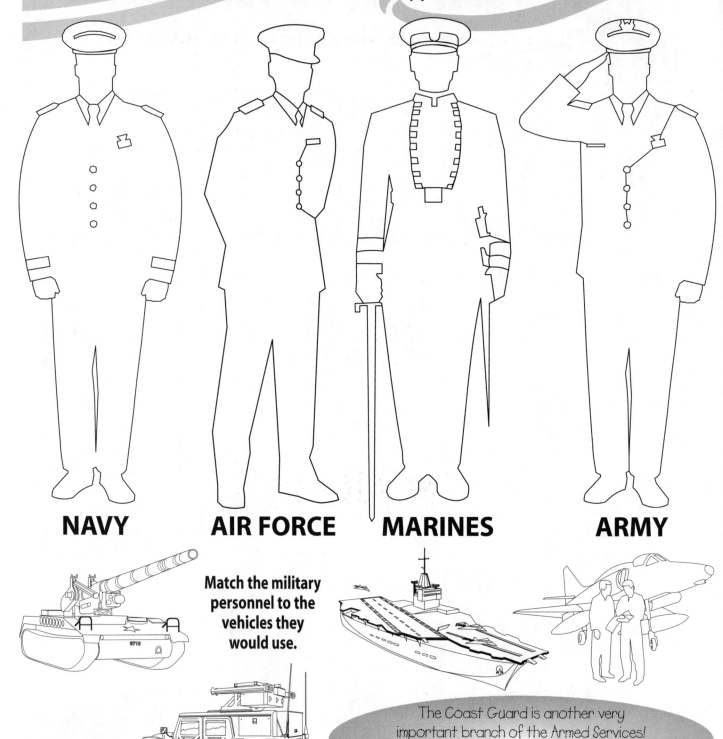

NAVY   **AIR FORCE**   **MARINES**   **ARMY**

Match the military personnel to the vehicles they would use.

The Coast Guard is another very important branch of the Armed Services! The Coast Guard personnel protects America's ports and coastlines!

  ©2001 Carole Marsh • Gallopade International • 800-536-2GET • www.gallopade.com • Page 30

A Capitol Criss-Cross!

The city where our nation's business is handled is the capital, but the building where important work for our nation is done is the *Capitol.* The Capitol is one of the major landmarks of our country.

Do the crossword puzzle below to find out more about the nation's capitol.

ACROSS

1. A statue named this is on top of the Capitol. It's something Americans value most.
4. The House of Representatives and the Senate are together called this.
6. In this large room in the Capitol, states have placed statues of some of their most famous people. The room is called _____ Hall.
7. Along with the Senate, Congress is also made up of the _____ of Representatives.
8. At the Capitol, Congress makes these.

DOWN

2. This big round thing on top of the Capitol is made of cast iron and weighs 9 million tons!
3. The Capitol is made up of 540 of these.
5. Congress is made up of the House of Representatives and the _____.
7. The Capitol sits on land called Capitol _____.

A Towering Patriot!

Starting with S, cross off every other letter to reveal facts about Abe!

S H B E R L I O P V M E W D I T F O Q R Y E Z A J D !

____ _____ ___ _____!

S H F E Z W M A H S W A K G D I I F P T V E B D E S R T K O L R E Y

G T O E C L W L O E X R .

___ ___ _ _____ _____.

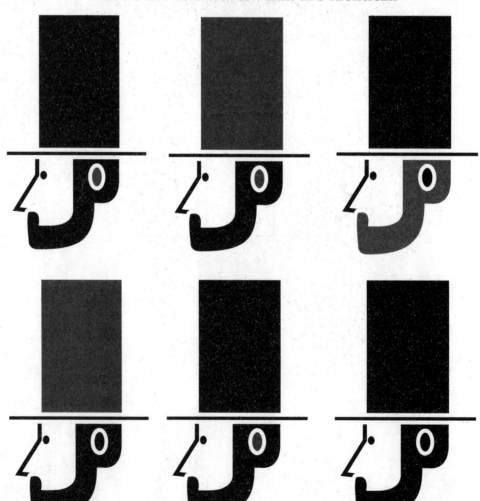

Circle the two "Abes" that are identical.

Let Freedom Ring!

Liberty Bell

The bell first cracked in 1753, when it was first tested. This was due to a flaw in the casting or the brittleness of the metal.

Since it was first hung in Independence Hall, the great bell has announced many important events.

Solve the math problems to find out the years in which the bell rang for freedom! (Hooray!)

1. The Liberty Bell summons citizens to hear the first public reading of the Declaration of Independence by Colonel John Nixon.

   8-7=   4+3=   10-3=   14-8=

2. The people of Philadelphia find out about the Stamp Act

   1+0=   18-11=   3x2=   25÷5=

3. The final expansion of the bell's crack occurs on Washington's Birthday.

   20÷20=   4x2=   16÷4=   12-6=

The inscription on the bell reads: "Proclaim Liberty throughout all the land unto all the inhabitants thereof." This sentence is Leviticus 25:10 in the Bible.

America's Helpers on Parade!

The United States Armed Forces are made up of the following branches:

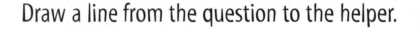

ARMY   NAVY   AIR FORCE   MARINES   COAST GUARD

If you have an emergency, you might call on another type of helper. Police officers, firefighters, and emergency medical technicians are ready around the clock to help people.

Draw a line from the question to the helper.

1. Who will you call if someone is breaking the law?

2. Who will you call if the house next door is on fire?

3. Who will you call if you see someone who is badly hurt?

4. Who will the nation call if the safety of the country is threatened?

Which of these helpers might fly the military jet below?

THE PURPLE HEART MEDAL!

The Purple Heart is the oldest military decoration in the world that is still in use. It was also the first award established for soldiers. George Washington created it for soldiers in the Revolutionary War.

The Purple Heart is awarded to troops who are injured in combat by an enemy of the United States. If the injured soldier dies, the Purple Heart is presented to a loved one.

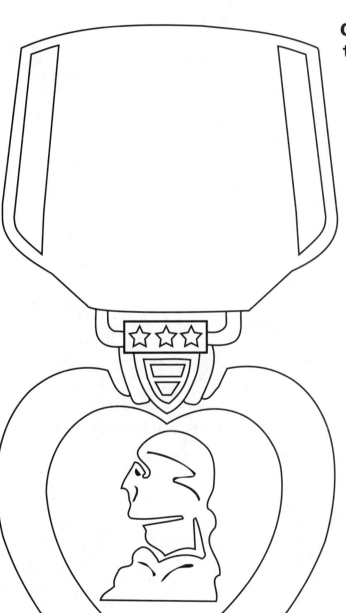

Color the Purple Heart medal using this description as a guide:

The medal hangs from a purple ribbon with two white stripes on the side. At the top of the medal is a shield with three red stars over two red stripes. On either side of the shield is a small patch of green. The outer heart and George Washington's bust are bronze (use a gold or light brown color). The heart shape around Washington is purple.

Use this outline to design a new medal! Cut it out and wear it.

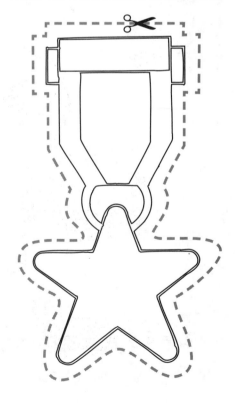

FAST FACT!

The Purple Heart costs more to make than any other military decoration in the world! It starts out as a rough bronze stamp of the heart and goes through 18 more steps to achieve its final appearance with its gold plate, colorful enamel, and purple and white ribbon.

As American as Apple Pie!

My, oh my, I love apple pie!
It's an All-American treat!
With cheese, if you please,
Or whipped topping (just a squeeze)
YUM! YUM! LET'S EAT!

Can you write a poem about your favorite All-American food? Maybe it's something your town or state is famous for—like Wisconsin cheese or Iowa corn or Georgia peach pie or Cincinnati chili. Are you hungry yet?

_____

_____

_____

_____

_____

_____

_____

_____

_____

_____

Celebration Cakes

For an All-American treat, make some cupcakes and frost them with white icing. Decorate them with blueberries or cherries or strawberries. Red licorice or fruit roll-ups make nice stripes! Or you could make an American flag sheet cake. Frost with white icing. Use sliced strawberries to make red stripes. Blueberries can be used to make the blue union and miniature marshmallows resemble the white stars! *Enjoy!*

Patriotic Puppets!

Cut out the faces of these founding fathers (and mothers) and modern-day patriots. Color them and glue them onto popsicle sticks. Write speeches for your puppets. Have them tell the stories of their part in U.S. history. Maybe you can have them talk about what they think of our nation today!

George Washington

Harriet Tubman

Benjamin Franklin

Thomas Jefferson

Susan B. Anthony

Jane Addams

Martin Luther King, Jr.

Abraham Lincoln

HAVE A PATRIOTIC PUPPET PARADE!

My Country 'Tis Of Thee!

America
("My Country, 'Tis of Thee")

My country, 'tis of thee,
Sweet land of liberty,
Of thee I sing.
Land where my fathers died!
Land of the Pilgrims' pride!
From ev'ry mountainside,
Let freedom ring!

Written by: Reverend Samuel Francis Smith 1832

Star-Spangled Sculptures!

With an adult's help, you can make your own play dough and use it to make models of important American symbols. How about a Statue of Liberty? A Liberty Bell? An eagle? What others can you think of?

Patriotic Play Dough

1 cup flour
1/2 cup salt
2 teaspoons cream of tartar

1 cup water
1 tablespoon oil
food coloring

Mix flour, salt, and cream of tartar in a saucepan. Combine water, oil, and food coloring in a small bowl. Add to saucepan, mixing well. While stirring constantly, cook over medium heat until mixture forms a ball. Remove from heat and allow to cool before kneading the mixture until it's smooth. To use more than once, store dough in an airtight container, or you can let your figures air dry and paint them in patriotic colors!

A Handy-Doodle Flag

Here's a fun and easy way to make an American flag.

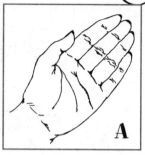

WHAT YOU NEED: A white piece of paper, a pencil, crayons or markers, and your hand

WHAT TO DO: Find a flat, smooth surface. Take one hand and with your fingers close together (see picture "A" on the right) lay your palm flat onto the piece of paper. Use the space on this page if you like. Trace around your hand with your pencil. Now, draw and color the "stripes" formed by your fingers red and white like the stripes on the flag (see picture "B" on the right). Draw and color the portion where your palm was blue.

Now, add stars. Can you fit 50 of them?

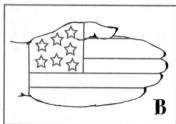

THE USS CONSTITUTION

The frigate *USS Constitution* is the oldest commissioned warship still afloat in the world. (You can't keep a good ship drydocked!) Both the vessel and the document for which she was named are lasting symbols of America's strength, courage, and liberty! During the War of 1812, a British soldier is said to have seen shot bouncing off the side of the *Constitution*. He shouted, "Huzzah! Her sides are made of iron!" After that, her nickname became "Old Ironsides."

The *USS Constitution* was sent to protect America from attacks by Barbary pirates, and the navigator's sextant fell overboard! Help her crew find their way home.

START

FINISH

A Patriot from the Past!

In the 1770s, many people came from England to make the American colonies their home. The king of England tried to control them by taxing even the tea that they drank!

Finally, the new colonists had enough! They decided to fight the mighty army of England! The colonists (who were now calling themselves *patriots*) grabbed their hunting rifles and threw on their tri-cornered hats! But could they win any battles? Unlike the British army, they didn't have many supplies or much training. But the *patriots* did have something very important: the desire to be free! *Guess who won the war!*

Look at the drawing of the patriot and draw a line from the word on the left to the part of his uniform it matches.

Musket

Boots

Hat

Belt

Knee breeches

Pack

As the Revolutionary War continued, more soldiers had to be trained. Men from many backgrounds waited to fight. When the call came to go to battle they had to be ready in a minute's notice. That's how they got the name of

____ ____ ____ ____ ____ ____ MEN

(Hint: There are 60 of these in one hour!)

Approved by the President!

The president of the United States uses a special seal to make documents official. It is on his stationery, medals, monuments, flags, and publications. It is even on the buttons of every soldier's uniform. You probably recognize the front side of the seal. It shows an eagle with an olive branch in his left claw and a bundle of arrows in his right. The olive branch symbolizes that America is mainly a peaceful country. The arrows show that when the time comes to fight for what we believe in, we're ready to do that, too!

Using the words in the word bank, find the hidden words that apply to the Seal of the President of the United States.

ARROW	PRESIDENT
DOLLAR	SEAL
EAGLE	SOLDIER
OLIVE	STAR

T	U	H	D	O	L	L	A	R
R	A	S	O	L	D	I	E	R
P	R	E	S	I	D	E	N	T
F	R	A	W	V	S	T	A	R
J	O	L	M	E	Y	E	X	Z
D	W	E	L	G	A	E	P	N

The last president to make a change to the seal was President Harry Truman. He turned the eagle's head to face left toward the olive branch. While America should be prepared for war, we should always look toward peace, he said. President Truman also added the 48 stars on the inner border of the seal of the number of states in the Union then.

SEALED DOLLAR BILL: President Franklin Roosevelt added the seal to the $1 bill in 1935. In fact, he put both sides of the seal on it. The back of the seal features a pyramid with an all-seeing eye at the top!

Monumental U.S.A.!

Oh, no!   A windstorm blew through our nation's capital of Washington, D.C., and the surrounding area. It blew the signs off some of the major monuments and memorials. A city employee is trying to match the signs with their proper monuments. Using the clues, please help.   The monuments that were affected are listed here:

Jefferson Memorial

Lincoln Memorial

Tomb of the Unknowns

Vietnam Veterans Memorial

Washington Monument

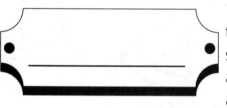

1. I am the monument that represents a president who led the country through one of its most difficult times: the Civil War. He lived long enough to see the war end, but his life was taken shortly after that. He sits inside me among 36 columns representing the 36 states that were members of the Union at that time.

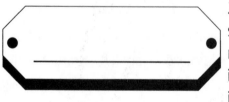

2. During the wars in which this nation has fought, many soldiers have died in service to their country.   Many times their bodies could be identified and returned to their families for burial. Sometimes, however, there was no identification. Since World War I, the remains of someone who could not be identified have been placed in me, a marble tomb.

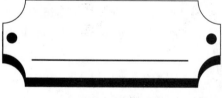

3. At 555 feet, 5 inches tall, I am the tallest monument in Washington, D.C. I honor our first president, the father of our country. Incidentally, there's no real proof that he actually chopped down that cherry tree!

4. Shiny black granite walls in the shape of a "V" form me, a unique monument. More than 58,000 names, 58,132, to be precise are inscribed in the granite. Can you find the sign that shares my name?

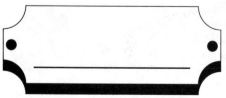

5. I am patterned after the home of our third president. A magnificent bronze statue of the president, who was most proud of his accomplishments as an architect and as an educator, is located inside me. By the way, he is also credited with penning the Declaration of Independence.

All-American Salad!

Here's a recipe for an All-American Fruit Salad you can make and enjoy with friends or family. It's just like America with all her ingredients (a melting pot of people!)

All-American Fruit Salad

1/4 cup maraschino cherries
1/2 cup blueberries
1/2 cup sliced strawberries
1/2 cup miniature marshmallows
1 banana, peeled and sliced
1/3 cup chopped nuts–pecans, walnuts, or peanuts
3/4 cup mayonnaise or mayonnaise-type salad dressing OR mix 1 cup plain or vanilla yogurt with 1/3 cup honey

Mix all ingredients in a large bowl, stirring gently to distribute the dressing evenly over the ingredients. Refrigerate until time to eat.

Ask one of your parents to help you prepare this tasty All-American dish.

EAT AND ENJOY!

Answer Page

PAGE 7

France; 214 crates; 408 steps in all; 10 years

PAGE 8

$44.68

PAGE 13

A-Missouri; B-South Dakota; C-Washington

PAGE 15

There are 13 eagles nesting on the mountain.

PAGE 16

7 red stripes; 6 white stripes; 50 stars

PAGE 18

salary; postage stamp; middle, initial; surveyor; cherry; wooden

PAGE 21

Bald eagle-1; Stars and Stripes-5; Liberty Bell-3; Uncle Sam-4; Statue of Liberty-2

PAGE 30

Answers will vary.

PAGE 31

ACROSS: 1-Freedom; 4-Congress; 6-Statuary; 7-House; 8-laws.   DOWN: 2-dome; 3-rooms; 5-Senate; 7-Hill

PAGE 32

He loved to read. He was a gifted storyteller. No. 1 and No. 5 are alike.

PAGE 33

1776; 1765; 1846

PAGE 34

1-police officer; 2-firefighter; 3-emergency medical person; 4-military officer;

military officer

PAGE 42

Minute

PAGE 44

1-Lincoln Memorial; 2-Tomb of the Unknowns; 3-Washington Monument; 4-Vietnam Veterans Memorial;

5-Jefferson Memorial